A Mom of Many Hats

by Debbie Fink, MA and Lisa Perea Hane, MFA
illustrated by Caroline Smith Heming

Published by

HARMONY HEARTH,® LLC
www.harmonyhearth.com

To all the moms and dads who have fought the fight, or are battling the battle;
and to their beloved children, for whom this heartfelt book is written.
From our hearts to yours,
Lisa, Debbie, and Caroline

To our families who supported our efforts through their love and patience.

Wholehearted thanks to all the individuals, families, and institutions that helped
make this project a reality. We could not have done this without your help.
It takes a village.

Published by
HARMONY HEARTH,® LLC
www.harmonyhearth.com
Bethesda, MD
Printed in the U.S.A.
ISBN 978-0-9678871-3-5

A NOTE TO ADULTS

This book's purpose is to help children cope with a parent who is battling cancer and undergoing chemotherapy. The combined storybook/chapter-style book is written for children of varied ages. Each child can experience the story in an age-appropriate manner. Each family can then use this book as a tool to discuss the cancer journey. Cancer treatments take time. The book's content and length are intended to assist the family during this time. An adult should read the story prior to reading it with a child. Here is how to read the book with:

Pre- and early readers
Follow the pictorial story. Limit the storytelling. Answer questions simply.

Readers
Follow the textual (and pictorial) story. Answer questions age-appropriately.

All children
Read Part One (The News, pp. 5-21) in one sitting. Read Parts Two and Three in several sittings. Know when enough is enough. Continue at another time.

Children often experience fear and the loss of normalcy while a parent battles cancer. Coping with this loss has many stages, such as: Shock; Denial; Depression; Regression; Anger; Bargaining; and Acceptance.[1] Every experience is different. There is no formula for the order, duration, or number of stages experienced. Hence, each stage is imbedded in this story, opening the door for dialogue with the child.

Shock:	Brad, pp. 8, 11; Olivia, pp. 8, 9, 11	Regression:	Brad, pp. 11, 12; Olivia, p. 12
Denial:	Brad, p. 8; Olivia, pp. 8, 11	Anger:	Olivia, p. 12; Dad, p. 12
Depression:	Brad, p. 23; Olivia, pp. 9, 15, 17, 23	Bargaining:	Brad, pp. 11, 21
	Mom, p. 16; Dad, p. 7	Acceptance:	Brad and Olivia, pp. 18 – the end

[1]Adapted by Debbie Fink, M.A., from Kubler-Ross, E. (2005). *On Grief and Grieving: Finding the Meaning of Grief Through the Five Stages.* NY: Simon & Schuster.

A special thanks to oncology social worker Elaine Goodrich Chase, LGSW, for her professional input.

PART ONE
The News

PART TWO
Party Day

PART THREE
From Fear to Strength

PART ONE
The News

"Mom, I'm home!" My annoying, younger brother Brad and I had fought the whole walk home from swim practice. Steaming mad, I was in a bad, ugly, angry mood. Brad spent all our ice cream money, my friend won every race we swam, and I lost my bathing cap – again! I could already hear Mom scolding, "Olivia, you have to be more responsible for your things . . ."

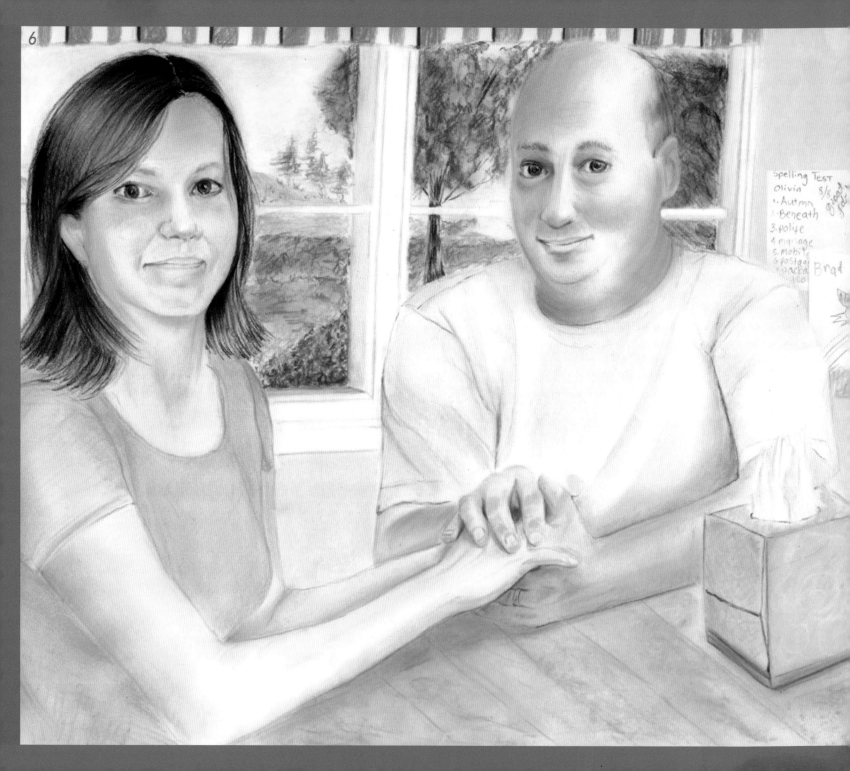

Halfway into the kitchen, I was surprised to see Dad at the table, holding Mom's hands. Why was he home this early? Mom's eyes looked puffy and red, and she tried to smile, but it seemed fake. They both looked like they'd been crying.

Dad got up and hugged Brad, saying, "Brad and Olivia, go change into dry clothes and meet us in the living room."

I looked at Brad, and we both shrugged. My anger over the ice cream money quickly melted. What was it that they wanted to talk about?

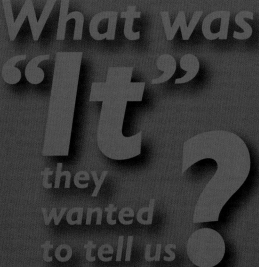

What was "It" they wanted to tell us?

"It" was that our mom had cancer. We couldn't believe It.

"It"

Mom and Dad tried to talk about **"It"** to help us understand.

They explained **"It"** for what seemed a long, long time—

the science of **"It,"**

the treatment of **"It,"**

the *if you want to talk about* **"It,"**

the *we're here to listen and to explain* **"It."**

"It" was all a blur.

"Its" name is cancer.

Poof.

In that moment, I felt as if all the colors of the rainbow had been washed away, turning my world both upside down and into shades of gray.

The conversation continued. Dad explained, "After her surgery, Mom will start chemo."

"Isn't Keemo a game show?" Brad interrupted. I rolled my eyes. Leave it to Brad to be funny without trying.

"No," Dad answered, smiling. "Chemo is short for chemotherapy. It's medicine that kills cancer cells. And it'll make Mom's hair fall out."

"So you'll be bald like Dad?" I asked.

"Yup. We'll be like matching salt and pepper shakers. But my hair will grow back," Mom responded.

Brad asked, "Who will be the salt and who will be the pepper?"

Later on, Mom and Dad didn't stop Brad when he stuck his thumb in his mouth, which he hadn't done in a really, really long time.

I felt frozen inside. I hear what they're saying about Mom, but she *looks* fine. This can't be happening!

It must be a bad dream. Maybe I'll wake up soon, and everything will be back to normal.

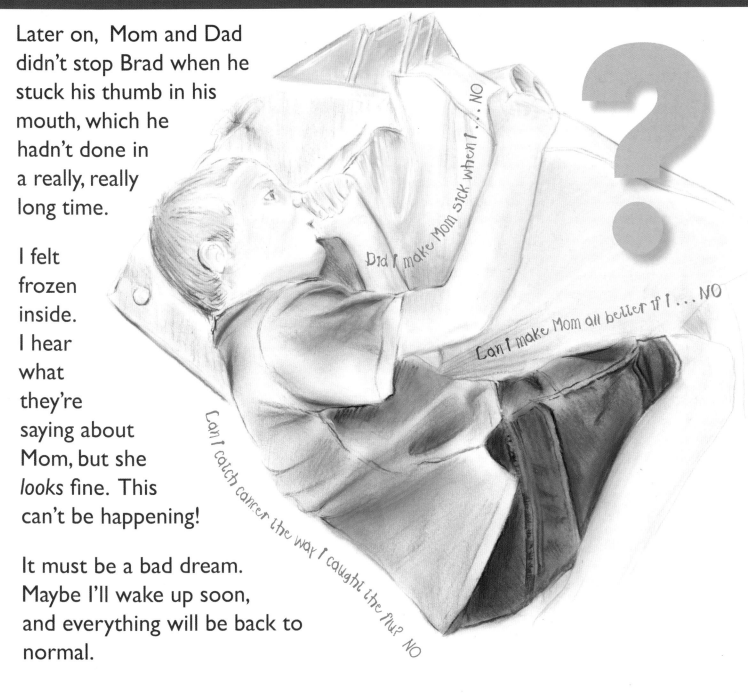

Did I make Mom sick when I . . . NO

Can I make Mom all better if I . . . NO

Can I catch cancer the way I caught the flu? NO

The next several weeks were like a slow motion *roller coaster* ride on a rainy, gloomy, gray day.

Nope.
I wasn't
dreaming.
The next
several weeks
were like a slow
motion roller coaster ride on a rainy, gloomy,
gray day. The high point was when Grandma arrived.
The low point was Mom's surgery.

Brad and I talked to Grandma about Mom's cancer, about
our arguments, about silly and stupid and serious stuff. Like
the time I flipped out for no good reason. She explained to me:
"Honey, it's normal to feel angry. That's the cancer talking."
So *that's* why Dad lost his cool out of the blue the other night.

Grandma was always cooking and baking and humming. She even
hummed as she changed and washed our bed sheets morning after
morning. We cooked and baked and hummed along with her.

Mom predicted that soon after she started chemo, her hair would begin to fall out. It did. Not a little at a time, but in clumps. She looked like the family cat after a fight with the dog next door.

Finally, Mom asked Dad to take her outside, and to gently shave off the rest. He did.

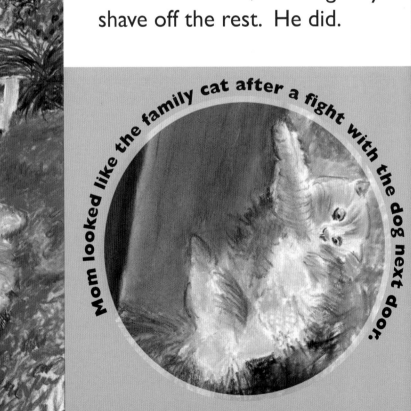

Mom looked like the family cat after a fight with the dog next door.

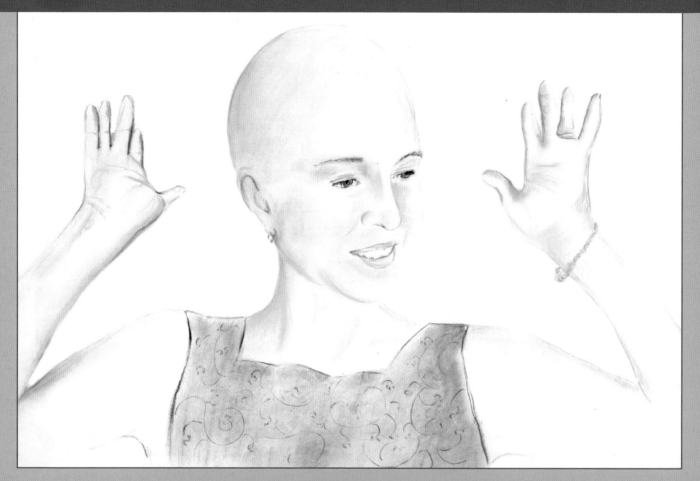

There she stood, her head shiny and different. She looked like an actress in a science fiction movie. "I never knew your head was such a pretty shape," I commented as I ran my hands over her bald head. Her head felt so smooth and warm. The feeling under my palms reminded me of the times I rubbed Mom's belly when she was super pregnant with Brad.

"You could be a department store mankin!" exclaimed Brad.

Laughing, Mom reacted, "I think you mean *mannequin!*"

We tried very hard to live our normal lives. Dad went to work. Brad and I hung out at the pool. But I didn't really *feel* normal.

One morning I woke up early from yet another bad dream. I heard someone crying. "Mom?" I whispered.

Mom stood staring at herself in the mirror. I had never seen her look so tired and sad. It scared me. My heart felt so heavy. She was surprised to see me, and tried to smile.

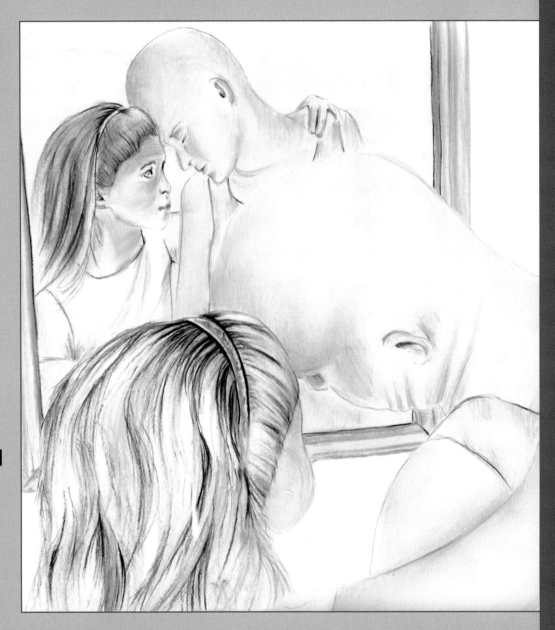

"Oh, Olivia," she confessed, embracing me in a big bear hug. Her salty tears dropped on my sunburned arm. "I'm feeling so ugly, and I'm just tired of being tired. I don't mean to feel sorry for myself, but sometimes I get fed up with all of this!" She sighed and wiped her eyes.

"I'm sorry Mommy. I love you." I kissed her tearstained cheek. It felt strange to be doing the comforting, as if, in that moment, Mom were the child and I were the mom.

Mom was hurting, and it made me sick to my stomach. I sat in the lonely living room. I thought and thought until my brain hurt.

I ached for my old mom. I need her "back in the saddle," as Uncle Carl would say.

Uncle Carl . . . who sent Mom her favorite sunflowers before surgery . . . I thought about all the folks in Mom's life who love her and want to help. Her friends, neighbors, and family are her rainbow of happiness. Mom was always doing things for them – like the baby shower she threw for her friend –

Then it came. The Idea. A Brilliant Idea. "Yessss!" I shouted and shot up like a firecracker.

A Hat Shower! It will rain hats – a shower of hats, all colors, shapes, and sizes – just like the baby shower! But instead of raining baby gifts, it will be pouring hats! I giggled as the idea spilled over me.

Brad and I would throw Mom the happiest hat shower ever! We could help Mom – who said she felt ugly – feel beautiful again.

A Hat shower! It will rain hats – a shower of hats, all colors, shapes, and sizes

Heading straight for Brad's room . . .

I pounced on his bed, woke him up, and announced my idea. Slowly, Brad's grin grew from ear to ear. He dashed to his desk, grabbing crayons and paper. It didn't take us long to make a super invitation.

We snuck downstairs to find Dad at the computer. Giggling, we shared our idea. A smile slowly spread across Dad's face.

He checked Mom's chemo appointments, and chose a good day for the party: Saturday, July 18th — two weeks from next Saturday. What a magical, delightful, delicious day July 18th would be!

Next, we eagerly showed Grandma the invitation. She loved it! Grandma dabbed her eyes and yelped, "Well? Let's get going – we have a party to plan!"

From then on, when Mom napped, we worked on the party. I was surprised by how much there was to do!

Brad spent two Sunday afternoons collecting colored comics from our neighbors' newspapers.

We had such fun turning the comics into party hats for our guests. Brad announced, "These are our Super Silly Laughing Party Hats." I think Brad hoped his hats would magically make Mom all better.

PART TWO
Party Day

Party Day finally arrived. The plan was for Dad to take Mom out for breakfast with their friends, followed by a brisk walk, and then to bring her home for the surprise. We could hardly wait for them to leave!

Brad was so excited that his cheeks turned as red as his shirt. Mom looked worried, and felt his forehead for a fever. I was so scared she'd figure out our plan. Dad practically pulled Mom out the door.

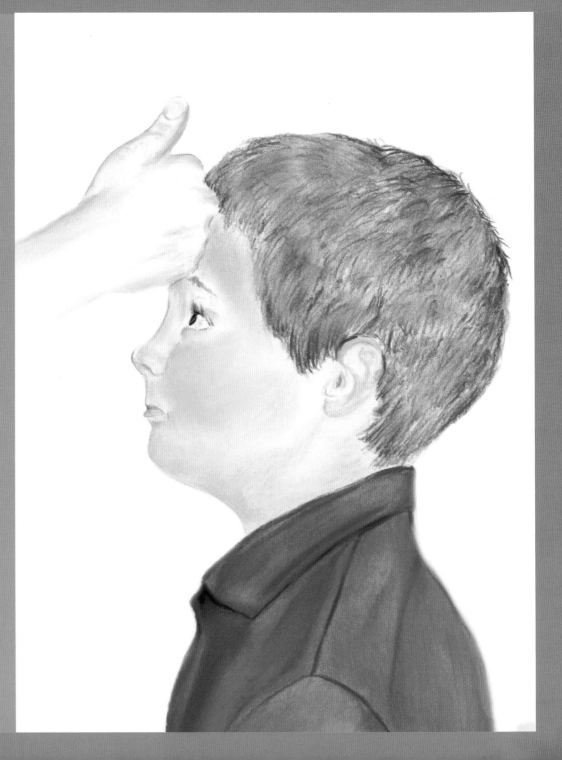

It's the first time in a long time that my heart isn't hurting!

When the door closed, I turned to Brad, ready to scream. "Sorry!" begged Brad. "I couldn't help it. It's the first time in a long time that my heart isn't hurting!"

Again, my anger melted away. "Yeah," I whispered. "It's the first time in a long time that *my* heart isn't hurting, either."

blueberries

broccoli

tea

reD grapes

Dark chocolate

ANTIOXIDANTS

Brad, Grandma, and I charged into action. We moved furniture, decorated Mom's "magical chair," and were super busy in the kitchen. Baby Bro Brad even had the cool idea to serve heaping bowls of blueberries and broccoli, our favorite antioxidants. Everything looked, tasted, and felt great!

Right on time, our guests arrived with hats in hand. They waited in the living room, whispering excitedly. Once all the guests were gathered, I snuck outside and yanked the sign off the door.

Sssh! Enter Quietly

At Your Own Risk! ☺

GO TO Living Room

and put on your super silly laffing party hat!

Eventually, we heard voices and laughter outside. The front door creaked open and then slammed shut. As Dad steered Mom and their breakfast friends in our direction, we all yelled . . .

I had the perfect view to soak in this most perfect moment. Mom's jaw dropped like a wooden yoyo, her eyes opened like two boardwalk lollipops, and her body froze like a bronze statue. As if it were a picture from a scrapbook, I knew this moment would stay with me forever.

Mom stared at her guests, who were all wearing Brad's goofy party hats, while Dad led her to her magical chair. She was speechless.

Tapping my glass with a spoon to get everyone's attention, I gathered my courage and announced, "Mom, this is a Hat Shower for you. We all think you're beautiful the way you are – "

"You're right about that!" interrupted Dad.

So let the hat shower begin!

I quickly continued, " – but we decided that you could use a loving boost to get you through the rest of chemo and beyond. And we're sick of seeing you in old baseball caps and worn out bandanas. So we're giving you hats! It's a shower of hats!"

"Lots and lots of hats!" Brad chimed in. Next, he proudly explained to Mom, "Each guest's hat stands for something you'll need to get through this yucky cancer. You'll see what we mean really soon!" Brad then blurted, "so let the hat shower begin!" Everyone clapped and cheered.

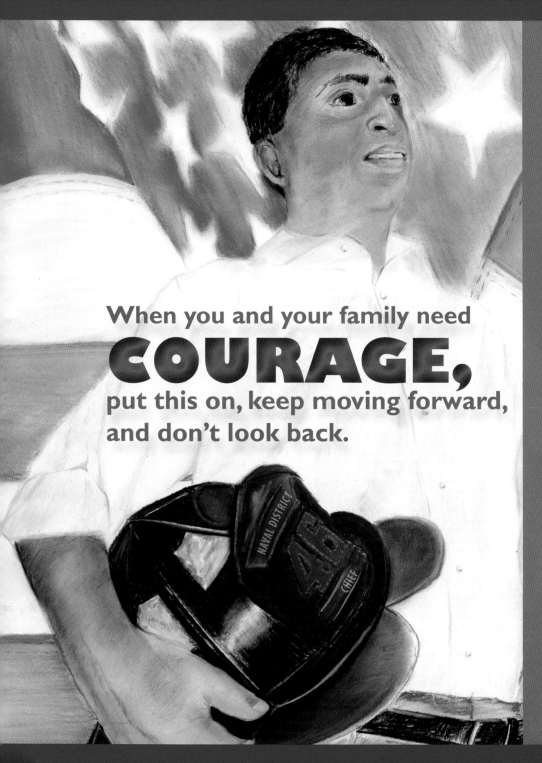

When you and your family need

COURAGE,

put this on, keep moving forward, and don't look back.

"I'd be honored to go first," announced our neighbor, Rahul, in his super deep voice.

It was no surprise that Rahul was first to step forward, since he's a courageous fireman and retired Marine.

"I give you this fire hat." He placed it on Mom's head. "You take care of it. It's given me courage each time I've charged into a burning building. So when you and your family need courage, put this on, keep moving forward, and don't look back."

"Why, thank you, Rahul," choked Mom. "I'll – *we'll* – take all the courage we can get!"

Then Tina, famous in our community for performing on Broadway years ago, rose to her feet. Mom once took a drama class from Tina at the local theater, and they became fast friends.

With great flair, Tina slowly drew out the most dazzling, razzmatazz, sequin top hat from behind her back.

BROADWAY

STARRING

TINA!

TINA!

"Darlin', my days on Broadway were never easy, and countless times I wanted to quit. But I kept pushing onward. I persevered. And was I ever so happy I did."

PERSEVERANCE is the theme of this act. The show must go on!

Tina paused dramatically, stared Mom straight in the eyes, and declared, "That's what you have to do now. Perseverance is the theme of this act. The show must go on! With this top hat, babe, you'll keep fighting. With attitude."

Mom smiled at Tina, winked, and blew her a starry-eyed kiss.

Next, Uncle Carl, who lived on a ranch, sidled up to Mom. My imagination lassoed his ranch and dragged it right into our living room! "Li'l sis," he said, "you know this hat's my favorite. When you're feeling wobbly and need to regain control, slide into this ol' cowboy hat. Climb back in the saddle and hold on tight to your reins. And remember I'm always here for you. I love ya, sis."

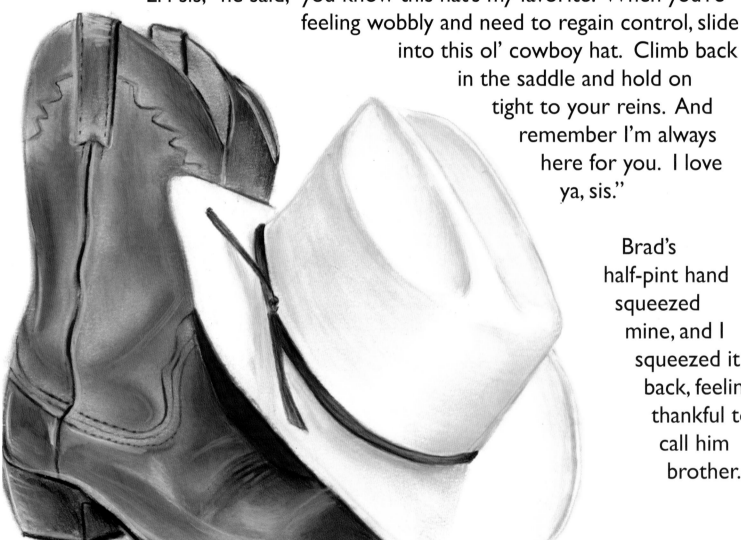

Brad's half-pint hand squeezed mine, and I squeezed it back, feeling thankful to call him brother.

When you're feeling wobbly and need to regain CONTROL, slide into my favorite ol' cowboy hat.

Brenda O'Brien (we call her "Mrs. O"), Brad's baseball buddy's mom, then bounded up. Immediately, I remembered that Mrs. O had battled breast cancer, and Mom organized meals and carpools for the family.

Mrs. O now tossed a baseball cap into Mom's hands.

Shaking back her thick hair, Mrs. O boomed in a voice that could rattle windowpanes, "Sister, been there, done that. I hereby replace your old baseball cap with this new one. It's the cap of hope. So when you or your family need a dash of hope, grab this cap. Then roar, 'Batter Up!'"

Catching the cap mid-air, Mom gave Brenda a thumb's up, and coolly placed it backwards on her head.

PRINCIPAL

WELCOME

Next up was Mom's childhood friend Mr. Lee. "Don Lee? You're in on this, too?" Mom asked.

They had been friends since second grade. Mom told us about their silly pranks, which often landed them in the principal's office. Mr. Lee – who is now a school principal! – pulled out a weird Viking hat.

THE POWER

"Remember how our high school was called Home to the Vikings? Well, with this Viking hat, you'll feel as powerful as we did back in high school. Wear this when you need the power to fight like a Viking and conquer your world!"

Brad plunked it on his own head, and it practically covered his nose!

TO FIGHT LIKE A VIKING

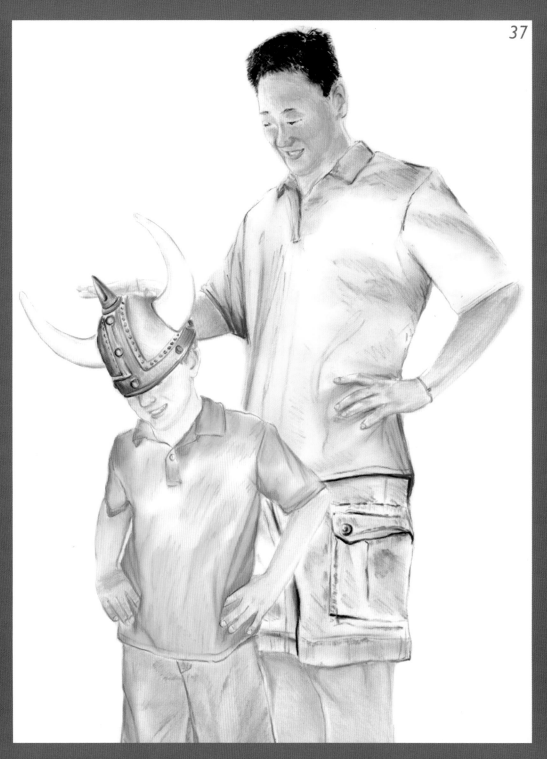

FAITH

~~DOUBT~~

Healing Powers

During all the joyful noise, Mrs. Charleston cautiously rose and stepped towards Mom. It was as if she were outside, carefully tiptoeing around hidden Easter eggs.

She and Mom run the church's clothing drives for local homeless families. Quiet Mrs. Charleston only has kind words to say about everyone.

She always smells of my favorite lavender soap and wears the very same bonnet to church every Easter.

Mrs. Charleston pulled out her Easter bonnet. I couldn't believe she was handing it to Mom! "My dear, whenever you're feeling doubt, just put on my well-worn bonnet. It'll remind you that faith has healing powers."

"Thank you, I will," whispered Mom.

Talkative Tova took her turn. Mom and Tova work in the same office, and Tova knows a lot about wigs. Her sister Barbara even owns a wig shop. Tova's also super funny, and always makes Mom laugh.

Today she pulled out a ravishing red wig from a soft, satiny bag. Red??? I gasped. But Mom's hair is brown!

"Honey, the office pitched in to purchase this fine and fashionable wig. You'll have such fun as a redhead! Wear this when you need a good laugh or an ounce of humor."

"Well," Mom blurted between giggles, "tell them at work that a fun-lovin' redhead will be taking my job!" I was beyond embarrassed when Mom turned and winked at Dad!

Wear this when you need a good LAUGH or an ounce of HUMOR

Santiago smiled as he stood up. Santiago owns Mom's favorite market, and sells the freshest produce in town. He held an enormous, crushed velvet sombrero in his gigantic hands. He bought the sombrero on vacation many years ago.

"*Escuchame, mi amiga (listen, my friend),* you always make my day, coming through my store's doors with something sweet to say. This sombrero, a symbol of my country, should remind you to relax and rest when you need it. As hard working people, we have no time for *siestas (afternoon naps).* But I want **you** to take *siestas.* And your family can use some extra rest, too.

Mom gave Santiago a humongous hug. "*Gracias,* Santiago. I – *we* – sure will rest up!"

Relax and Rest when you need it

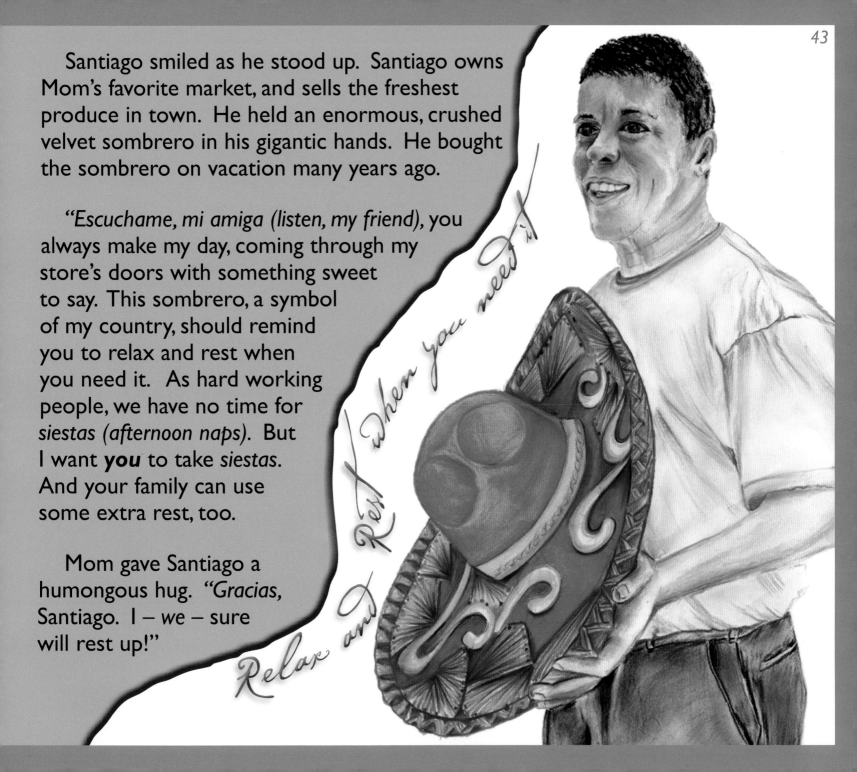

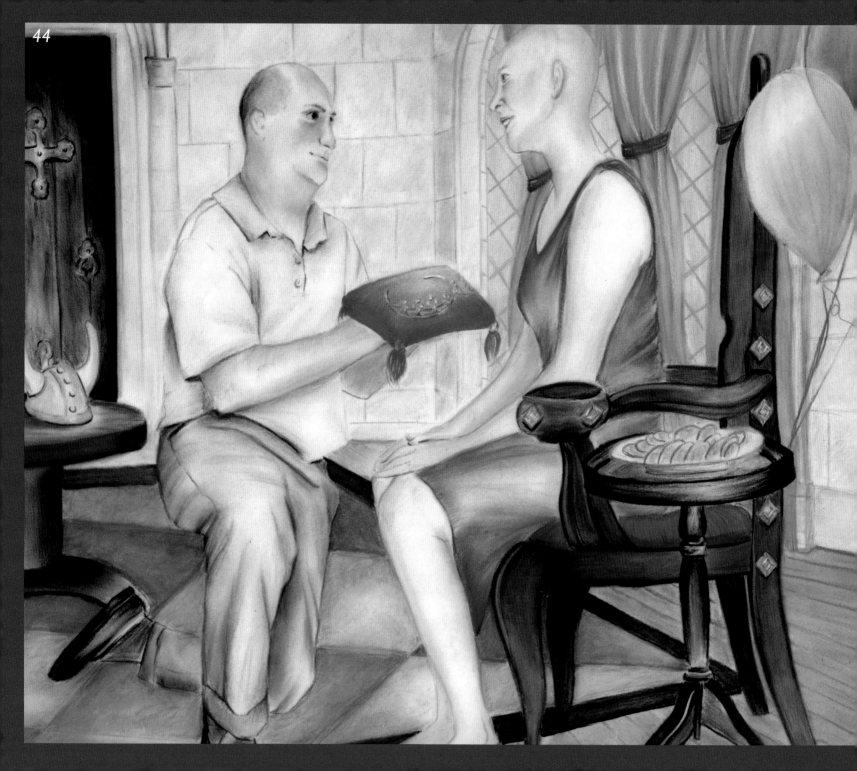

Next was Dad. In a flash, I blinked and my imagination converted our living room into a medieval castle chamber. Kneeling down on one knee, Dad fumbled for his gift and tenderly held it out to Mom.

In sickness and in health

Beauty

Mom gasped as she gingerly lifted a sparkling, studded, silver tiara from its plushy, tasseled pillow.

Dad cleared his throat. "You're beautiful, inside and out. Whether you have brown hair or red hair or no hair at all, you are the most exquisite woman in my world."

The room was silent except for sounds of sniffles. Mom whispered so softly that I could barely hear: "And you, my love, are the most princely, noble man in *my* world."

Wow … it seemed as though Cupid himself had swung in on a sunbeam and struck them both with one fling of an arrow!

Mom! I found it–

the cap of RESPONSIBILITY.

As time stood still, I snuck out and grabbed my bathing cap from its hiding place. I ran up to Mom, waving it in my hand.

"Mom! I found it – the swim cap I lost at the beginning of the summer! I've learned to be more responsible. Here! It's the cap of responsibility."

Mom kissed me on my head. She then stretched the ugly cap over her bald head, crowning it with the beautiful tiara. She looked hilarious! Everyone laughed aloud.

FEAR STRENGTH

Mom was too choked up to speak, between her tears and her laughter. Brad then plunked one of his goofy party hats over her tiara and bathing cap, and the sound of everyone's laughter bounced off our walls! We hugged each other, knowing in our hearts that we had learned to face our fears head on, and found the strength to do so as a family.

PART THREE
From Fear to Strength

The shower part of the party was over. I held Mom's hand and Brad held her other hand while she paraded around the room. Every now and then she squeezed my hand and smiled at me. I felt as though a special fairy had sprinkled her magical dust on all of us.

Our guests drank fruit punch and ate everything we'd prepared. Brad's antioxidants were a huge hit! Dad pulled out his camera and snapped lots of photos of everyone making new friends, catching up with old ones, and trying on all the different hats.

Not once did Mom look the teeniest bit sad – just very happy and beautiful.

As guests said goodbye, Mom placed one of Brad's party hats on their heads and thanked them for coming. We were relieved when the last guest left, but felt lighthearted and pleased, too.

We sure did live every moment of today to its fullest!

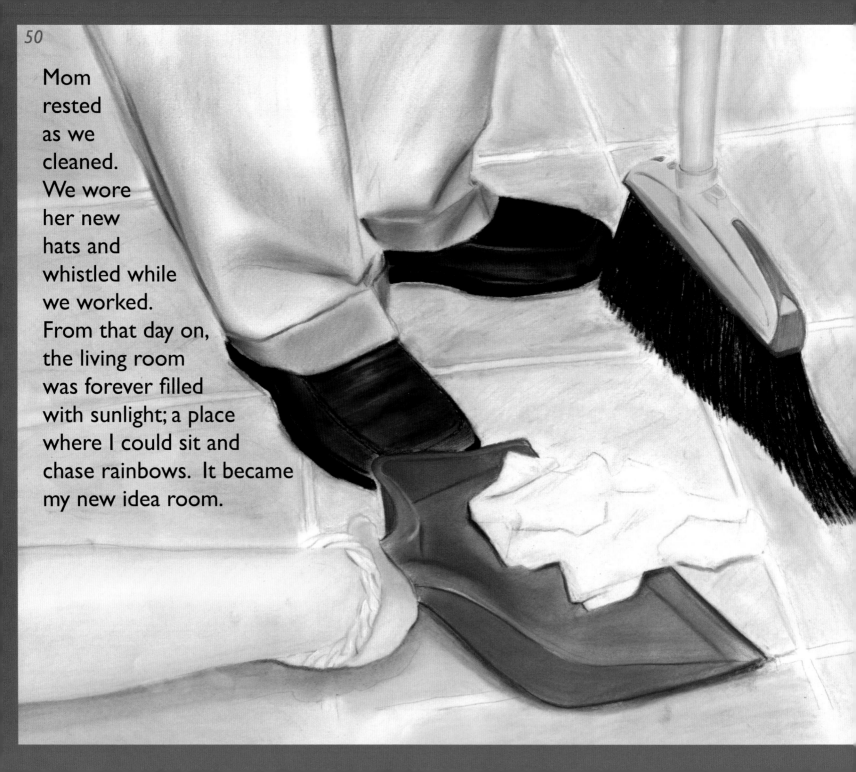

Mom
rested
as we
cleaned.
We wore
her new
hats and
whistled while
we worked.
From that day on,
the living room
was forever filled
with sunlight; a place
where I could sit and
chase rainbows. It became
my new idea room.

A few days later, Dad hung the photos on our fridge: Photos of Tina swapping stories with Mrs. O and Mr. Lee; Grandma hugging Uncle Carl; Mrs. Charleston talking with Rahul; Santiago laughing with Tova; and Brad wearing the sombrero while dancing with Mom.

We love those photos! They show us what kids can do when we put our minds and hearts to work. Today our kitchen overflows with smiles, reminding us of our perfectly awesome party day.

Life keeps rolling right along . . .

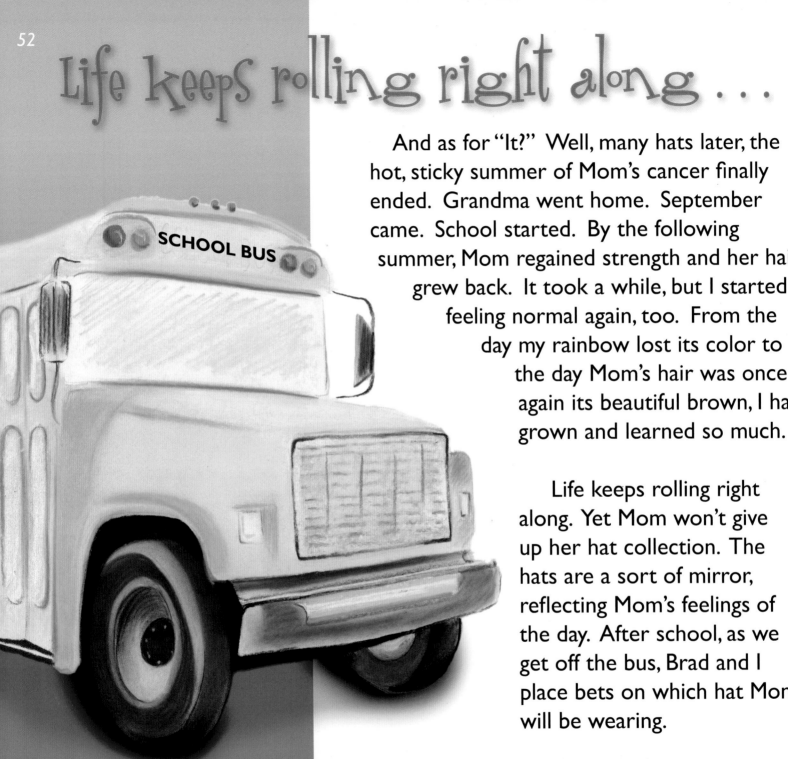

SCHOOL BUS

And as for "It?" Well, many hats later, the hot, sticky summer of Mom's cancer finally ended. Grandma went home. September came. School started. By the following summer, Mom regained strength and her hair grew back. It took a while, but I started feeling normal again, too. From the day my rainbow lost its color to the day Mom's hair was once again its beautiful brown, I had grown and learned so much.

Life keeps rolling right along. Yet Mom won't give up her hat collection. The hats are a sort of mirror, reflecting Mom's feelings of the day. After school, as we get off the bus, Brad and I place bets on which hat Mom will be wearing.

Mom is always happy to share her hats. On days when one of us needs some . . .

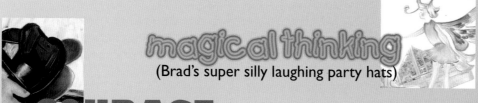

magical thinking
(Brad's super silly laughing party hats)

PERSEVERANCE
(Tina's top hat)

COURAGE
(Rahul's fire hat)

Hope
(Mrs. O's baseball cap)

CONTROL
(Carl's cowboy hat)

POWER
(Don's Viking hat)

Relaxation
(Santiago's sombrero)

HUMOR
(Tova's red wig)

FAITH
(Mrs. Charleston's Easter bonnet)

Beauty
(Dad's silver tiara)

RESPONSIBILITY
(you guessed it – my bathing cap)

. . . we slip into the right hat, and without words, the family knows
how we feel, what we need, and tries to make it better.

Hunt for these helpful words on the different party guest pages!

So that's how life changed. Any time I think about Mom's cancer and our summer of the hats, two words come to mind:

M E

W E

Flip the word ME, and it becomes WE. It was the summer I woke up to see that WE are so much stronger than little ol' ME.

We were so relieved when our super awesome mom once more became a Mom of Many Hats, doing Mom Things and being there for all those moments that fill our lives with rainbows of color.

And We journeyed on "hattily" ever after!

There are many ways besides throwing a hat party to help a parent feel better. What might work for you and your family? Find a trusted person (a family friend, teacher, relative, counselor, or neighbor) you can talk with to come up with an idea that feels right for you and your family. Please visit www.momofmanyhats.com for more ideas, resources, and child-friendly activities.

ABOUT THE CREATORS

DEBBIE FINK (left)
is an author, educator, and performer who has written numerous scripts and books. She creates meaningful, inspirational experiences. Her books, workshops, and performances reach readers and audiences domestically and internationally. Debbie and her husband have three children.

LISA PEREA HANE (center)
is the inspiration behind this story. As a mom with Stage 4 cancer, she wanted to write a children's book that celebrated each of life's moments. Lisa and her husband have three children.

CAROLINE SMITH HEMING (right)
is an internationally recognized graphic designer and illustrator. Her inspired illustrative work herein is in memory of her dear friend, Tracy. Caroline and her husband have three children, two cats, a dog, a fish, and two frogs.

Debbie, Lisa, and Caroline live in Maryland with their families.

Our hearts are with you on your journey . . .